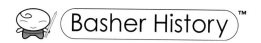

LEGENDARY CREATURES

KINGFISHER

LONDON & NEW YORK

KINGFISHER
LONDON & NEW YORK

First published 2021 in the United States by Kingfisher
120 Broadway, New York, NY 10271
Kingfisher is an imprint of Macmillan Children's Books, London

Author: Mary Frances Budzik
Consultant: Lizanne Henderson
Editor: Anna Southgate
Designer: Dave Jones
Proofreader: Dolores York

Dedicated to Jasper and Alienor Niquette

Distributed in the U.S. and Canada by Macmillan,
120 Broadway, New York, NY 10271

Library of Congress Cataloging-in-Publication Data has been applied for.

ISBN: 978-0-7534-7753-3 (Hardcover)
ISBN: 978-0-7534-7754-0 (Paperback)

Kingfisher books are available for special promotions and premiums.
For details contact: Special Markets Department, Macmillan, 120 Broadway,
New York, NY 10271

For more information, please visit www.kingfisherbooks.com

Printed in China
9 8 7 6 5 4 3 2 1
1TR/0721/WKT/RV/128MA

CONTENTS

Introduction
Legendary Creatures

We didn't exist, so you humans decided to invent us.
Good call! Many centuries ago, you guys opened the
floodgates of your imaginations and set us free to roam in
a pretty wild world. We play by our own rules now—we're
a cabinet of curiosities, a shape-shifting menagerie gone
rogue—and we're ready to slink, pounce, flap, soar, hoot,
howl, holler, and (in some cases) eat you up. No offense!

In classical myths, all the big players are shape-shifters
or hybrid monsters (or both). We rampage through the
illustrated pages of medieval bestiaries and menace
the deeps charted on Renaissance maps. As Christianity
prospered, we often were identified as having a close
relationship with the devil, cursed with cloven hooves,
horns, and pronged tails. During the Age of Exploration,
we symbolized the dangers lurking in uncharted lands.
And during the era of European colonial expansion into
Africa and Australia, hunters with the heebie-jeebies told
tall tales of bizarre cryptid creatures that some people
still insist are out there somewhere. Maybe, maybe not.
We aren't telling; it's all part of our mystique!

Chapter 1
Water Creatures

We're as different as the water bodies we inhabit. Mokele-mbembe and the Loch Ness Monster wallow in swamps and prehistoric lakes, revealing mere glimpses of their bodies, whereas Mermaid and Hippocamp are publicity-savvy ambassadors for the briny ocean. Guardian nature spirits Mishipeshu and Naga use their powers to keep their watery homes pure, while Kraken leads sailors to mistake its bulk for a landmass. Beware cucumber-craving Kappa, icicle-fingered Qalupalik, and that bad-boy of the billabongs, Bunyip. These sinister types will work their dark magic to lure you under the watery ripples.

Mokele-mbembe

Kappa

Naga

Bunyip

Hippocamp

Kraken

Loch Ness Monster

Mermaid

Qalupalik

Mishipeshu

Kópakonan

Encantado

Mokele-mbembe

■ Water Creatures

✳ Brontosaurus-like creature from the Congo River basin, Africa
✳ This monster's name means "one who stops the flow of rivers"
✳ Said to burrow nests into the clay that builds up in river bends

I'm a Congolese swamp thang with a mucho murky myth. Like my long-lost Scottish cousin, the Loch Ness Monster, I've found that playing hard to get makes you humans just that much more determined to track me down. Since my first reported sighting, at least 50 expeditions have tried to bag my bod. One was even sponsored by the Smithsonian museum!

My virtual *WANTED* poster describes me as the size of an elephant, brownish gray, and snaggle-toothed. I've got a small head, long neck, clawed toes, and a thick, muscular, dino-ish tail. Man-eater? Not me! I graze on liana vines. Pathetic, I know, but my enormous size means that I'm bad news to canoes. . . Oh, and I hate hippos! Those guys snatch all my plant munchies!

● This creature's native Likouala Swamp region is the size of New York State
● Early European reports mention enormous three-clawed footprints
● First reported sighting by a European: 1776, by a French missionary

Mokele-mbembe

Kappa
■ Water Creatures

* ✳ Japanese water monster whose name translates as "river child"
* ✳ This monkey–turtle hybrid can be either scaly or slimy
* ✳ Real-life inspiration: Japanese giant salamander

Want to be my pal? Show me the cucumbers! They're my fave nosh. I'm a greenish river monster with a shallow hole in my head and a turtlelike shell on my back. I can set broken bones, sumo wrestle, and irrigate fields! How's that for a diverse array of talents? And the hole in my head? It's called a *sara* (dish), and it contains sacred water; if it spills, I lose my powers.

Kappa

* ● Kappas pull horses into water to drown them; they dunk humans, too
* ● To keep bathing spots safe, Japanese kids toss cucumbers into the water
* ● Dangerous swimming areas are often marked with a sign showing a kappa

Naga
Water Creatures

* Indian nature spirit portrayed as half human, half cobra
* Common to Hindu, Buddhist, and Jain mythological traditions
* *Naga* is the Sanskrit word for "serpent"

Naga

Charm me! I am a snake, after all. Twined around a lichened tree trunk or slithering over the cool stones of an old water well, I am the spirit guardian of pure, natural places. Respect the environment, and I'll bring gifts of rain or fertility. Pollute my sacred spaces at your peril, however. My gentle rain will become a disastrous flood or disappear completely in a drought.

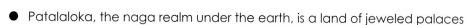

● Patalaloka, the naga realm under the earth, is a land of jeweled palaces
● Female nagas are very beautiful; some Indian royalty claim naga ancestry
● A naga enemy, the mythic bird Garuda, pursues nagas during a drought

11

Bunyip
■ Water Creatures

✻ This amphibious monster lurks in Australian swamps
✻ Its name means "devil" in the aboriginal Wergaia language
✻ Also known as the kianpraty or wowee

I mess with people's minds. They find my appearance so bizarre that they can't agree on what they see. Here's one report: a bloated seal, starting to melt around the edges, is wrapped in an old shag rug that needs vacuuming. Not pretty! Another says I'm 4–6 feet (1.2–1.8 meters) long, with a round bulldoggy head, rheumy popping eyes, prominent ears, stubby tusks, flippers and/or claws, and more droopy folds of hairy hide than a shar-pei dog.

Nobody has anything good to say about me. Even the water I'm said to favor is stagnant. I just love billabongs (river backwaters formed by flooding). My signature call is a dissonant yowl, and I'm happy to chow down on any human foolish enough to set foot near one of my squishy hideouts. I just need to hug them to death first . . .

● The bunyip features in aboriginal "dreamtime" (origin myth) lore
● European reports of this creature's existence date back to 1845
● The word "bunyip" is used in Australia to mean "impostor"

Bunyip

Hippocamp
■ Water Creatures

✸ Half horse, half fish; a creature from ancient Greek mythology
✸ The name is from Greek *hippo* (horse) *kampus* (sea monster)
✸ It is said to have been created from the crests of sea waves

Stampede at sea! Poseidon, my sea god master, loves my high spirits. I am his loyal steed, with the noble head, arched neck, and muscled torso of a thoroughbred horse, coupled to a curved sea serpent rear. No hairy tail to swish at flies, but my pronged whale tail sure does the trick with pesky minnows. My mane is often shown as a fin instead of horsehair, and my hooves are made not of horn but of web.

My snorts send up bubbles from my pastures deep beneath the sea. Seaweed is good grazing! Poseidon rides me bareback or hitches several of us to his chariot and uses his trident instead of a whip to urge us on. When we paw the waves with our finny hooves, the sea kicks up foam and spray. It's a maritime rodeo!

● The hippocamp originated in Greece and Phoenicia (now Lebanon and Syria)
● Hippocamp mosaics often decorated public baths in Rome
● The hippocampus in the human brain resembles the creature—hence its name

Hippocamp

Kraken
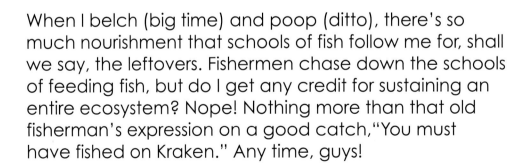
■ Water Creatures

✷ A gigantic tentacled creature from Nordic maritime lore
✷ Inhabits the seas around Norway, Iceland, and Greenland
✷ Aka Hafgufa (sea mist) or Soe-Trolden (sea mischief)

I'm a big guy and proud of it. When my back breaks the sea's surface, sailors yell "land ho!" They think they've just discovered a new country! From the earliest accounts in Icelandic sagas, I've been described more like a landmass than a living creature. I get gripes about the wakes I create when I surface or submerge—swells and whirlpools that reach for miles, sinking ships as they go.

When I belch (big time) and poop (ditto), there's so much nourishment that schools of fish follow me for, shall we say, the leftovers. Fishermen chase down the schools of feeding fish, but do I get any credit for sustaining an entire ecosystem? Nope! Nothing more than that old fisherman's expression on a good catch, "You must have fished on Kraken." Any time, guys!

● The kraken was reported in the Greenland Sea as early as 1250
● It is mentioned in *Moby Dick* and a Tennyson sonnet, "The Kraken"
● Naturalists speculate that the creature may be a giant squid

Kraken

Loch Ness Monster
Water Creatures

* A giant dinosaur-like monster inhabiting Loch Ness, Scotland
* Also goes by the more familiar name of Nessie
* Distant cousins: Nahuelito (Argentina) and Champ (Canada)

Nessie! Such a cute name for a monster, no? I'm an ancient beast, too, first sighted by Saint Columba, a monk from the Scottish island of Iona, back in the year 565. I poked my head up for air, but the intrepid monk zapped me back to the depths of my loch by making a hasty sign of the cross. It was a long way down, too—around 788 feet (240 meters) of deep murkiness due to silt runoff from Scottish highland streams. What a hideout!

Some think I'm a plesiosaur, a marine reptile from the late Cretaceous period. But despite centuries of observation from the ramparts of ancient Urquhart Castle on the banks of the loch and many sonar-scan snoops in its watery depths, I've revealed only tantalizing bits of myself—a serpentine neck, a humped back, and my small, shy head.

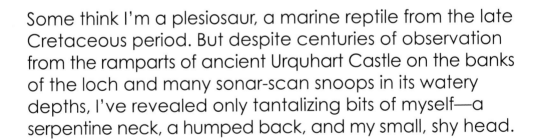

● Nessie tourism contributes millions of dollars a year to the Scottish economy
● The monster has its own animated Google doodle
● A famous photo of Nessie (1934) was a fake dinosaur head fixed to a submarine

Loch Ness Monster

Mermaid
■ Water Creatures

✳ This water spirit is half woman, half fish
✳ Mermaid tales surfaced around 1000 BCE in ancient Assyria
✳ Name combines Old English *mere* (sea) and *maid* (maiden)

You know me—long, wavy hair (that I like to comb), slinky fishtail, eternal youth . . . well, have you ever seen a wrinkly, gray-haired mermaid? Greek sailors thought we were omens of shipwreck, and when Columbus spotted us near Haiti back in 1493, he complained that we weren't as pretty as he had expected! What end of the spyglass was he looking through?

Mermaid

● Mermen are said to exist, but they have never been as popular in myth
● Circuses once exhibited Fiji mermaids—a stuffed monkey/fish combo
● Pearls and sea glass are sometimes called mermaids' tears

Qalupalik
Water Creatures

* This humanoid monster is a feature of oral Inuit tradition
* Said to live under the ice in lakes and Arctic seashores
* Wears an Inuit *amauti* (pouch) on its back

Qalupalik

I'm a humanoid female with long dripping hair, algae-scummed, scaly skin, and a sulfurous reek. I help Inuit parents keep their children safe, because my fearsome legend scares them away from treacherous ice. If I can snatch you up, I'll snuggle you inside my *amauti* and take you away to my underwater igloo. Then I'll feed off your energy to stay immortal.

- Robert Munsch's children's story *A Promise Is a Promise* features a qalupalik
- Inuit women use an *amauti* to carry babies on their backs
- Monsters with sacks who steal children are common to many cultures

Mishipeshu
■ Water Creatures

☀ An underwater panther of North American Ojibwe tradition
☀ Inhabits Lake Superior (called Gi Chi Gamiing by the Ojibwe)
☀ *Mishipeshu* means "great lynx"

I'm a panther on the prowl, lurking in my underwater lair. Every swipe of my webbed paws and lash of my super-long tail beneath Lake Superior's waters whips up whirlpools of dark energy. The Ojibwe people blame the lake's dangerous rip currents, sudden violent storms, and ice volcanoes on my fits of catty craziness.

I'm no ordinary feline. I have horns like a deer, and my spine is spiked with copper blades for slicing through the lake's thick winter ice. For thousands of years before the Europeans arrived, Native peoples dug copper deposits around my lake to make tools. When industrial-scale mining began in the 1800s, many ships carrying copper ore were wrecked on the lake. The Ojibwe pinned the mishaps on me, saying I was offended by such large-scale theft. Meow!

● Pictographs of Mishipeshu are painted on Agawa Rock by the lake's shore
● Charms made from Mishipeshu's copper bring good luck to Native hunters
● Mishipeshu joined the thunderbirds to fight for a balance of power over nature

Mishipeshu

Kópakonan
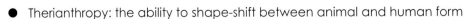 Water Creatures

- ☀ A shape-shifter from the Faroe Islands, Denmark
- ☀ Shape-shifts to a human by removing its skin
- ☀ Male or female, the Seal Woman has the best-known story

I'm a human woman who drowned at sea and found new life as a seal. On the enchanted 13th night of the year, my seal friends and I shed our sealskins, shape-shift back to our human forms, and dance on the beach. A farmer spied on me, stole and hid my skin, and took me to live as his wife. When, finally, I found my skin, I returned to my seal form and my beloved sea.

Kópakonan

- ● Therianthropy: the ability to shape-shift between animal and human form
- ● A statue of the Seal Woman stands in Mikladalur on the Faroe Island of Kalsoy
- ● Other human/animal shape-shifters include selkies and swan maidens

Encantado
Water Creatures

* This Amazon river dolphin shape-shifts to a man at full moon
* *Encantado* translates as "enchanted or charming one"
* A flashy dresser, this guy is never without a stylish hat

Encantado

A tip of my straw boater and my secret's out— I hide my blowhole under there, you see, and need it to breathe. That's right, I'm more than just a human hunk—I'm also a very dapper dolphin. When the sambas start at Brazilian beach bashes, I shape-shift from dolphin to man and step ashore to charm the ladies. If I can, I whisk them down to the Amazon river bottom!

* Encantados have prominent foreheads, similar to dolphin "melons"
* They are often depicted as being pink in color
* When they shape-shift back to dolphin form, the hat stays on!

Chapter 2
Winged Creatures

High and mighty? That's us. We hang out with forces of the universe—thunder, lightning, and fire—but we often use our powers for good: Simurgh's tail feathers heal with a tickling touch, and Alicanto's gleaming eyes light the way toward rich veins of gold. Impundulu and Thunderbird trouble the air with the dark drumroll of thunder, while little Phoenix is the most mystic of all, resurrected from the flames of its own destruction. We put on a vibrant display as we whoosh through the air on our errands of magic and mercy: our red, gold, and purple plumages give sunrises and sunsets a worthy rival.

Basilisk

Impundulu

Garuda

Longma

Simurgh

Alkonost

Phoenix

Thunderbird

Alicanto

Dragon

Firebird

Oozlum Bird

Camazotz

Basilisk
Winged Creatures

✸ Featured in European medieval bestiaries (books of beasts)
✸ Had a rooster's head, a dragon's wings, and a serpent's tail
✸ Another name for the basilisk is cockatrice

The conditions of my birth were not ideal. Hatched by a snake from an egg laid by a rooster and buried in a dung heap (cozy)! Did you expect I'd grow up to be a cuddly pet? Hah! I'm lethal and proud of it. My smell, breath, hiss, and especially my glance will fry you in an instant.

I'm a popular image in heraldry (coats of arms). On 28 fountains throughout the city of Basel, Switzerland, I'm the dude with the head, legs, and beak of a mangy rooster and a reptile tail. Don't forget the scaly wings. The devil and I are best bros, and naturally any good warrior wants to kill me. There's only one way—if I see my own reflection, I'm ashes. Alexander the Great once forced me to gaze at myself in a mirror while defending a city. I died, of course, and the city was left open to attack.

● The ashes of a basilisk were prized by medieval alchemists
● Alchemists used basilisk ashes in a brew to try to turn base metal into gold
● The ancient Romans believed the basilisk's breath created the Sahara desert

Basilisk

Impundulu
Winged Creatures

✳ Lightning bird of South African Zulu and Xhosa folklore
✳ Said to be the spirit of dark thunderclouds
✳ A passion for milk is the impundulu's fatal weakness

I'm a bird bolt of bad news from the blue. The flapping of my charged-up wings sends shock waves that create thunder. To some, I appear as a lightning strike, but witch women (*sangomas*) see me for what I am, a crested white bird with red wings and shanks, and a dagger-shaped beak like a lightning rod. My flights are electrifying—no wonder South Africa is a world hotspot for lightning!

When I zap the earth with a flash and crackle, I deposit my eggs in the ground. Sorcerers prize them, grinding them into a powder that shines in the dark. It has the power to make lightning strike an enemy. But because my fat is a useful ingredient in all types of putrid potions, sorcerers also seek to capture and kill me. Those meanies lace milk (my favorite drink) with deadly herbs as bait.

● In some legends, witches have impundulus as their familiars
● Impundulu eggs are said to be found in craters caused by lightning strikes
● Wild mushrooms that appear in the rainy season foretell the impundulu's arrival

Impundulu

Garuda
Winged Creatures

* Part human, part bird of prey in Hindu and Buddhist traditions
* This demigod is associated with heaven, sun, fire, and victory
* *Garuda* means "eagle" in Sanskrit

Just call me Gold Feather! I'm a defender of good. After a 500-year incubation, I burst free of my mother's egg in a fiery blast and grew to enormous size in an instant. I soon won my mother Vinata's (mother of birds) freedom from enslavement to her sister Kadru (mother of snakes). Remember the Water Creature Naga? Well, the experience of my mother's captivity shaped me as a force for good, and I've been Naga's bitter enemy ever since.

I can take on any task and bear any burden—my outstretched, winged arms and hands form the *abhaya* gesture, the symbol for "have no fear." My proudest role is as the *vahana* (bird steed) of Vishnu, the Hindu god who destroys evil. Together we swoop through the skies as an elite duo, striving for good.

● In Hindu art, Garuda has a man's body with an eagle's wings, talons, and head
● Garuda is the national emblem of Thailand; Indonesian airlines is named for him
● Carvings of Garuda serve as supports at Angkor Wat temple, Cambodia

Garuda

Longma
Winged Creatures

* Half dragon (*long*), half horse (*ma*) from ancient China
* The neighing of a longma is as sweet sounding as flutes
* It can endure rides of 300 miles (480 km)

Put me though my paces! You'll be totally impressed. I can swoosh through the sky, gallop over the ground, and even trot on top of water. And if you happen to be an ancient Chinese emperor, legend has it that I can also grant you immortality.

The story goes that my mother was an ordinary mare who became pregnant by a water dragon when she waded in the Zi River. I got the best of both worlds—a horse's body and head, flanks armored with dragon scales, and scalloped dragon wings. The markings on my curly-haired back caught the eye of Fu Xi, one of the three sages of ancient China. The intriguing pattern of my spots inspired him to invent the mystical symbols that, one way or another, led to the development of Chinese calligraphy.

* Chinese military called a horse taller than 8 feet (2.4 meters) a *long* (dragon)
* Jade carvings of longmas bear scrolls to symbolize the link with calligraphy
* In a 4th-century text, Jin Emperor Mu travels in a carriage drawn by eight longmas

Longma

Simurgh
Winged Creatures

☀ Giant female bird of Persian (modern-day Iran) myth
☀ Often shown as a peacock with a dog's head and lion's claws
☀ Said to be large enough to carry an elephant in her talons

Light as a feather? Not this bird! At first glance, you might notice my ostrich neck, my fearsome talons, or my sheer size (my name means "30 birds," after all). But really, I'm all about my long tail feathers, which reflect the entire color spectrum. They heal wounds with a single touch. Then there are my wings! I live on the sacred Alborz mountain, atop Gaokerena, a tree with super-charged seeds. The downdraft from my beating wings scattered the seeds, germinating all the world's plants. You're welcome!

I'm fierce, but I'm not mean. In one legend, I took in a child called Zal, abandoned on my mountaintop by his cruel father. The boy's crime? Having white hair! I raised him on choice bits of prey, and now noble Zal is a popular hero of the Iranian people.

● Simurgh's favored food is sheep fat
● A good omen, she appears on the shoulder of kings and powerful clerics
● She is said to have witnessed the destruction of the world three times over

Simurgh

Alkonost
Winged Creatures

✹ Woman-headed bird of Russian tradition
✹ Known for her mesmerizing, hypnotizing voice
✹ Has a sister, Siren, a creature with a darker nature

With the plumage of an exotic bird but the face of a woman, I draw all eyes as I ride the winds. And my chirps? They're spellbinding! Men drop everything to listen—and that's all they do, forevermore. They become bewitched.

My nesting site is Buyan, a magic island that slips undersea at high tide. When I get the timing right, my eggs roll right to the depths. While they incubate, I glide, sweeping my wings over the sea for seven days of calm—but when my babies break free of their shells, I rejoice by stirring up a violent storm. Great fun, but I can't stick around to watch the sailors suffer. I'm off to orchards to tend the apple crop. One sweep of my wings to brush dew off the apples, and they become fruits super-charged with healing powers!

● In Russian art, Alkonost is portrayed in orchards, singing
● Her name may come from Alcyone, a Greek demigoddess of the wind
● Siren, Alkonost's sister, is related to the Greek Sirens

Alkonost

Phoenix
Winged Creatures

※ Eagle-sized red, gold, and purple bird with a plumed tail
※ Its mythical origins date to ancient Egypt and, later, Greece
※ This ancient creature is associated with the sun and rebirth

Farewell, till we meet again! How well I understand the bittersweet emotion of those words! Bitter, because I am about to explode into flames. Sweet, because I shall rise from my own ashes, reborn, a mere fledgling. I build my own pyre atop the date palm tree, from twigs, cinnamon bark, and perfumed resins of pine and myrrh.

My legend is truly ancient. In the earliest stories, I would mysteriously appear every 500 years in Heliopolis, the Egyptian city of the sun. I came carrying the ashes of my father in a casket I molded myself from myrrh. My association with the sun evolved into my tale of rebirth through flame. Some say I ignite through the heat of my own body and fan the flames by the beat of my wings. And as I burn, I sing my own dirge, a sweet lament.

● Phoenix tears have healing powers and are an antidote for basilisk venom
● Legendary relatives include the Egyptian Bennu and the Chinese feng-huang
● Feng-huang is associated with Chinese empresses and is immortal

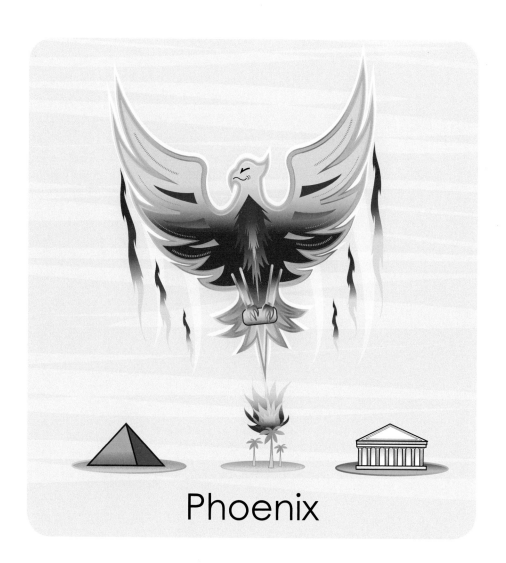

Phoenix

Thunderbird
Winged Creatures

* Gigantic bird or sky spirit of North American myth
* Can split open trees with its beak to find insects to eat
* Known as binesi by the Chippewa, animikii by the Ojibwe

When the skies turn a leaden blue-black, watch for me. I'm a conductor of the upper atmosphere, the boss bird whose great wings wave like bad-ass batons to inspire the forces of the universe to show their stuff. Boom, crackle, rumble . . .

I'm a sky spirit sacred to North American Native peoples from Maine to the Great Plains. They keep a weather eye out for my thunderclouds; I bring the rainstorms, which make grass grow lush for sacred bison. Yet my flashing eyes spark lightning, which can scorch that grass. On ancient petroglyphs (rock carvings), I'm carved in profile to emphasize my awesome wingspan and fearsome beak. I make my home in rocky nests on the highest mountains. My talons are so strong that I can pick up caribou or even whales to bring back home for dinner. Very tasty takeout!

● A common image in prehistoric petroglyphs throughout North America
● May be a cultural memory of the teratorn, a huge prehistoric bird
● In Ojibwe mythology, thunderbirds live on a floating mountain in the sky

Thunderbird

Alicanto
Winged Creatures

* Luminous nocturnal bird of Chilean legend
* Has a hooked beak, long legs, and talons
* Often weighted down by the metal ore filling its crop

Birdseed? Who needs it? I have more valuable things to peck at—like gold and silver ore! I'm an enormous bird with bright eyes and a metallic sheen. When I leave my mineshaft nest to feed, my glowing wings cast an eerie light over the night sands of Chile's Atacama Desert. The bird-watchers waiting to catch sight of me are miners. They're hoping I'll lead them to a hoard of precious metals.

Maybe, maybe not! If my intuition tells me a miner is pure of heart, I might lead him to one of my richest feeding grounds. If my pursuer is driven only by a love of money, my golden glitter becomes a blinding light. When the flash dims, the greedy gold digger opens his eyes to find himself on a strange road, and only a prayer to the patron saint of miners will lead him home.

● The shells of alicanto eggs are made of the metal it has fed on
● Alicantos may lead a miner over a cliff edge or down an abandoned shaft
● Several mining companies are named after the alicanto

Alicanto

Dragon
Winged Creatures

✳ This creature features in legends across the world
✳ The name comes from Greek *drakonata* ("to watch")
✳ King Arthur's surname Pendragon is Welsh for "chief dragon"

It's hard to catch a break when you're a dragon. The ambition of every wannabe hero is to slay you. But I'm so much more than just a fire-breathing mega-lizard waiting to be slain by ambitious saints and knights! I've crept my way into the early tales of many cultures.

In my time, I've been a guardian of both wisdom and caverns of treasure. The all-knowing Delphic oracle of the ancient Greeks was protected by Python, a dragon born from the very slime that created Earth. In one Welsh tale, two dragons—one red, one white—created castle-construction headaches for an ancient king called Vortigern. Each time his fortress inside the mountain Dinas Emrys neared completion, the slumbering dragons caused it to collapse, and he had to start over. Again and again.

● A wyvern is a two-legged, armless dragon that breathes poison instead of fire
● Dragons' heads are said to contain draconite, gems of mystic power
● Early Christians associated the dragon's fire breathing with the mouth of hell

Dragon

Firebird
Winged Creatures

☀ A creature of Russian myth, aka *zhar-ptitsa* (heat bird)
☀ Its eyes glow like embers or glitter like crystal
☀ Known to drop pearls from its beak to give to the poor

My golden-red glow warms the frozen Russian landscape. Just one of my flaming feathers can light the way through a snowy forest. In a quest to prove his royal worth, the son of a tsar, Tsarevitch Ivan, tried to capture me for my fiery feathers. But his father was angered by his success, because I pecked at the golden apples of immortality in the imperial orchard.

Firebird

● Magic horses and wolves help the hero Ivan in his quest to capture the firebird
● In one variation of the legend, only those who love beauty can see the firebird
● The story of the firebird is the subject of a famous Russian ballet

Oozlum Bird
Winged Creatures

* A small bird with brightly colored feathers
* Features in the mythology of Great Britain and Australia
* Said to disappear completely within itself when startled

Oozlum Bird

I'm an aeronautical wonder—a bird who flies backward because he likes to know where he's been. There are wags who claim I fly backward in tight circles, until I disappear up my own backside. If that makes you laugh, enjoy. I say I'm involved in a physics experiment—can I collapse in on myself like a black hole? Against the wind! That's my motto!

* First mentioned in literature in the 1890s
* The only bird that can actually fly backward is the hummingbird
* An oozlefinch is the U.S. Army Air Defense mascot

Camazotz
Winged Creatures

☀ A bat-god of death and sacrifice
☀ Originated in the mythology of K'iche' Mayan peoples
☀ The name means "death" (*kame*), "bat" (*sotz*)

Wanna play ball? Not with me! Just ask Hunahpu, demigod hero of the K'iche', an ancient Mesoamerican tribe. He and his twin brother, Xbalanque, journeyed to the underworld, where they dodged my bloodthirsty bite by zapping themselves inside their trusty blowgun. When Hunahpu shoved his head out of the blowgun pipe to see if I was still flapping around, I cut off his head and tossed it into play in an underworld ball court.

With webbed winged arms and a vampire-bat snout, I brandish a sacrificial knife in one fist and a human heart in the other. The heart? My payback. You see, I traded the knowledge of fire to mortals in exchange for control over their armpits and waists. Smart deal? Not for them, as it meant I could slice open their torsos over sacrificial fires.

● Bat-infested caves near sinkholes were said to be portals to the underworld
● Xibalba ("place of fear"), underworld home of camazotz, featured a ball court
● In the K'iche' myth, losers in underworld ball games were sometimes sacrificed

Camazotz

Chapter 3
Monster Mash-Up

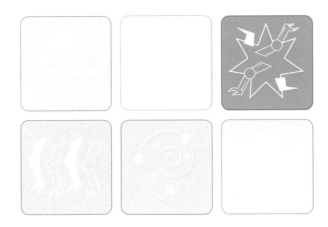

A dumbfounding bunch of mixed-up monsters, we have infiltrated the globe from the Indonesian rain forests to the New Jersey Pine Barrens. Weirdness is a way of life for us. Take Nue, who enjoys shape-shifting into a grim black storm cloud, or Bulgasari, whose favorite snacks include scissors and safety pins (ouch!). Then there's hairy Bigfoot, although you could ask what's so odd about him, since he does at least have two feet! And from 19th-century Europe comes omnivorous Ogre, a star of German and French fairy tales, despite having a face and figure in serious need of a major makeover.

Nue

New Jersey Devil

Bigfoot

Ogre

Ahool

Bulgasari

Nue
■ Monster Mash-Up

✳ This Japanese creature takes a variety of hybrid forms
✳ Can also transform into a swirling black storm cloud
✳ *Nue* means "night bird"; it is considered a bad omen

Did someone mix up the puzzle pieces? With a monkey's head, the mottled torso of a Japanese raccoon dog, tiger-striped limbs, taloned paws, and a reptile's scaly tail, I'm the grab-bag monster of your baddest dreams. Even my trademark mournful cry is a mash-up of shriek, wail, and whimper: hyoooo.

In a story from way back in 1153, when the Emperor Konoe had constant nightmares, a royal samurai spotted a threatening storm cloud hovering over the palace. He shot an arrow into the center of the black cloud and out I tumbled, slain! The emperor recovered his health and the villagers put my body out to sea on a barge. When my corpse washed ashore downstream, some cautious folk gave it a courteous burial to ward off my curse.

● Stories featuring nues date back to 12th-century Japanese folktales
● Nues are said to favor lonely spots such as decaying cities and remote villages
● An alternative description has a fox's tail, a cat's head, and a chicken's torso

Nue

New Jersey Devil
■ Monster Mash-Up

✳ A mythical leathery-winged creature from New Jersey
✳ Has a kangaroo's head, cloven hooves, and a forked tail
✳ Also known as the Leeds Devil

Hopping like a bird, my eyes burning with an eerie glow, I haunt the Pine Barrens, a coastal New Jersey forest once rumored to be inhabited by pirates. Perhaps you have heard my ear-splitting screams?

So the local legend goes, I was the unwanted child of real-life "Mother Leeds," a witch according to some. With 12 children already, Ma Leeds felt I was one too many, so she cursed me. She said I would be a devil (well, we all know that 13 is unlucky for some). My birth came on a dark and stormy night in 1735. As soon as I was born, I lashed my forked tail and made a swift escape up the chimney. On I fled through the dark of the night, until I reached the safety of the Pine Barrens . . . and I have stayed there ever since.

● In 1909, reported sightings of the creature led groups to hunt for it in the Barrens
● The sightings prompted a local to create a green, winged kangaroo as a hoax
● The TV show *The X-Files* once featured a story about the New Jersey Devil

New Jersey Devil

Bigfoot
■ Monster Mash-Up

✳ Elusive, wilderness-dwelling "man-beast" of North America
✳ Cousins include the yowie (Australia) and almas (Mongolia)
✳ Its Salish Indian name, Sasquatch, means wild or hairy man

Now you see me, now you don't. Playing hide-and-seek with my fan base has worked well; my media presence is awesome! In the world of legendary creatures, I'm the ultimate influencer, with thousands of reported sightings.

I'm around 8–10 feet (2.5–3 meters) tall, covered in mangy cinnamon-hued hair, neckless with bulked-up shoulders, and I reek! (Imagine ripe manure, burning rubber, and the subway . . . ahhh, eau de Bigfoot!) My tracks make craters big enough to bury a nosy human with a smartphone camera. I hang out in deep woods because that's where the grub is: it takes a forestful of acorns to keep me going, along with the occasional salmon snatched from a stream. My Asian cousin, Yeti, haunts the Himalayas—well, mountain goats are soooo yummy.

● Bigfoot makes noises described as screams, grunts, and whistles
● Some Indian legends describe bigfoot-types attacking livestock or humans
● In Canada, Sasquatch has his own postage stamp

Bigfoot

Ogre

■ Monster Mash-Up

✳ Tall, big-bellied humanoid monster of French origin
✳ Has wild hair and an out-of-control appetite
✳ An ogre's stupidity means the beasts are easily tricked

Down the hatch! My massive mouth is the trapdoor to a digestive dungeon for unfortunate victims. I like to feast on plump humans, with nice tender toddlers being a specialty! Given my high-calorie diet, it's no surprise that my weight is off the charts—I make football linebackers look delicate. My brain may be sluggish, but I always know when it's dinnertime!

Ogre ancestry is bad news, even when it's just a tiny, ancient trace! In the old French version of *Sleeping Beauty*, the queen mother had ogre relatives many generations back. Bad blood will out—she no longer looked ugly, but she was a secret, hungry ogress. She developed a craving to devour her own grandchildren, but her plot was foiled by a clever servant.

● Ogres featured in French author Charles Perrault's fairy tales (1697)
● The modern film character Shrek is an ogre, who can vent smoke from his ears
● Today, the word "ogre" describes someone who is cruel or frightening

Ogre

Ahool

■ Monster Mash-Up

✳ Legendary mega-bat from the Indonesian island of Java
✳ Has a primate face, gray fur, and an impressive wingspan
✳ Inhabits the deepest rain forests, roosting in caves by day

Tune right in to my bat beat, an awesomely wide-wing-beating, echoing sound located deep in the Indonesian rain forest. *Ahooool, ahooool*—that's my batty bleat. It bounces off cave walls, helping me find the perfect spot to hang (upside down, of course). Personally, I favor a hidden grotto with a waterfall view.

Nobody can decide whether I am a real or mythical figure. You see, I'm in a fight with skeptical scientists to prove I exist. Sightings of me have been few—no surprise, I'm the after-dark type! I did manage to convince the science nerds of this, though: it's the clicking sounds created by the beating of my 12-foot- (3.7-meter)-wide wings that allow me to find my way around. Like I always say, location, location, location. *Echo*location, that is.

● Echolocation is the location of objects by reflected sound
● The ahool is said to prey on fish but is rumored to have carried off humans
● A European cryptozoologist claimed to hear the ahool's cry in the 1920s

Ahool

Bulgasari
■ Monster Mash-Up

✳ A hybrid mythical beast from Korean mythology
✳ The name translates as "cannot be killed"
✳ An enemy of evil, a bulgasari devours bad dreams

I've got the original iron constitution! Feed me the contents of the kitchen sink—or the kitchen sink itself—and I can digest it. My guts are a scrap-metal heap.

Once upon a time, a Korean monk fashioned me from rice—a tiny creature who liked to eat needles, spoons, and scissors. If it was metal, I would munch it. I grew into a monster with an armor-plated hide, a bear's body (with needles for fur), an elephant's trunk, and a cow's tail. I can be melted down by fire, but I cannot be killed! In some stories, my greed for iron is a good thing, because I eat weapons of war such as swords and shields. In others, I protect humans by consuming their nightmares. But take care. If your bad dreams don't fill me up, I might gobble up your sweet hopes and dreams, too.

● Bulgasari is associated with starfish, which regenerate and so are hard to kill
● The creature is also said to defeat smallpox, once epidemic in Korea
● A 1985 North Korean film sponsored by ruler Kim Jong-Il featured a bulgasari

Bulgasari

Chapter 4
Four-Legged Beasts

Lucky for Unicorn and Kitsune that they are creatures of ancient pedigree and powerful magic, because their presence in this chapter puts them in some very bloodthirsty company! Quite a few of us are genetically programmed to hunt down a nice juicy meal, eat first, and ask questions later! From Manticore's stinger shooting to Chimera's blowtorch breath, we have some pretty impressive weaponry. Maybe the peaceable guys in this chapter could turn to Cadejo for bodyguard duty from the rest of us, but—would you put your trust in a mangy dog with glowing purple eyes? Hmmmm.

Nandi Bear

Ndalawo

Liqimsa

Kitsune

Manticore

Chimera

Hellhound

Pooka

Sphinx

Unicorn

Cadejo

Nian

Nandi Bear
Four-Legged Beasts

- A mythical nocturnal creature of African origin
- Has short ears, a stub tail, reddish or tawny hair, and claws
- Aka chemosit (devil) and gadett (brain eater)

Think my name sounds cute? Think again. Cuddling with me would be a catastrophe! I'm a lion-sized, slope-backed, long-armed carnivore with muscular shoulders, short hind legs, and a stubby, bearish snout. I lean forward on my knuckles as I lope my way through the dense Nandi Forest in the Great Rift Valley of Kenya. My valley is home to some of the earliest hominid fossils ever discovered. Did some of those early human ancestors stumble across my path? Bad luck—my favorite meal is brains.

I've never been captured or preserved, so zoologists can only guess at my physical form. Some think I may be the ancestor of the chalicothere—a prehistoric hoofed mammal with long front arms. Others guess that I'm a mishmash of hyena, honey badger, and aardvark.

- The Nandi bear is said to have a bloodcurdling howl
- European colonizers in Africa reported sightings in the early 20th century
- 1960s *Tarzan* comics showed the hero of the African jungle tackling the beast

Nandi Bear

Ndalawo
■ Four-Legged Beasts

☀ Extraordinarily ferocious predator of the Ugandan rain forest
☀ All black, except for its silvery-gray flanks and underbody
☀ The name means "dark leopard"

Say, maybe they need to name a sports car after me! It worked for the jaguar and the cougar—why not me? After all, I have a snazzy two-tone body, and I'm sleek and speedy with a menacing, ear-splitting squeal when I get revved up! One of the most mysterious and feared of legendary beasts, I'm the star of many a chilling tale told around campfires in Uganda's rain forests.

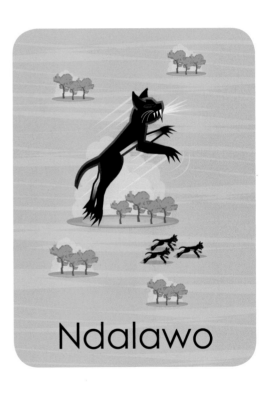

Ndalawo

- Sometimes mistaken for a hyena due to its crazy cackle
- Unlike the leopard, a solitary hunter, it hunts in packs of three or four
- It's thought ndalawos evolved pack hunting to survive as a threatened species

Liqimsa

Four-Legged Beasts ▪

* Elephant-like brothers of Ethiopian origin, both taller than cliffs
* They had club forefeet and human hindfeet, with toes
* Known as the swallowers due to their human-eating habits

Liqimsa

You'd think we'd know better than to trust the last words of someone we're about to devour. We'd gobbled up nearly every Borana warrior, before two brothers—one crafty, one brave—took us on. The crafty guy claimed his flesh would make whoever ate it immortal. As we fought over who was the most deserving, the brave brother speared us through our bellies.

● The liqimsas feature in the lore of the Borana Oromo people from Ethiopia
● The legend symbolizes the Borana people's clever defeat of rival tribes
● In a similar tale, the monster Dhuga is slain while rolling on its back to scratch mites

Kitsune
■ Four-Legged Beasts

☀ A shape-shifting fox spirit from Japanese folklore
☀ Some kitsune are friendly and helpful; others cause mischief
☀ A kitsune can grow as many as nine tails

A quicksilver fox spirit, I am a trusted deputy of Inari, the Japanese god of agriculture, rice, and prosperity. I can live to a great age, and as I grow older, my magic becomes stronger. Every hundred years, I grow a new tail and my pelt changes like the seasons from red to gold to wintry white.

In my fox form, I always keep my *hoshi-no-tama* with me, in my mouth or balanced on the tip of my tail. This glittering silver ball is the source of my magic power. Like any wily fox flitting through the forest, I weave in and out of Japanese culture. An enchanted groom might notice that his lovely young bride has a slender, pointy face and a foxtail twitching under her kimono. If he can steal my *hoshi-no-tama*, I will be an excellent wife because I will do anything to get it back. Without it, I will die.

● Kitsune first appeared in Japanese legends around 8 CE
● Physical clues to human fox possession include sharp teeth and small pointy ears
● Kitsune are related to Chinese nine-tailed magic foxes known as *huli-jing*

Kitsune

Manticore
■ Four-Legged Beasts

☀ A flesh-eating monster from Persia (now Iran)
☀ Had a lion's body, a human face, and a spike-tipped tail
☀ Its name derives from Persian *mar-tiya-khvara* ("man-eater")

My toothy smirk will set your teeth chattering in terror—
I've got three rows of sharp, serrated snappers, stretching
from ear to ear. Ears like yours, that is—my head and
face are eerily human, though I am the most savage
of beasts. My lionlike body is colored red, and my tail is
tasseled with scorpion stingers that I can fire off in a full
circle. If they miss their mark, no matter. Where they land,
they invade, sprouting overnight into a thicket of bristling
spears! A vicious spike tipped with fatal venom protrudes
from the center of my skull.

And yet . . . there are my eyes of baby blue and my
musical voice, like flutes and trumpets. Doesn't all evil
have just a little sweetness to tempt you to approach?
I'm part feline, after all. We love to play with our prey!

● The manticore is said to have consumed its victims' clothing, bones and all
● Legend has it that the beast could bend its tail in any direction when firing stingers
● Crushing the tails of manticore cubs supposedly prevented stingers forming

Manticore

Chimera
■ Four-Legged Beasts

☀ This female creature from Greek mythology has three heads
☀ A hybrid of lion (front), goat (middle), and snake (rear)
☀ Its name comes from a Greek word that means "she-goat"

Having trouble wrapping your head around the idea of me? Believe me, I sympathize! After all, I've got three heads, and none of them are exactly easygoing. In fact, my whole family is cranky: Mom was Echidna, known as the mother of many monsters, and my brother Cerberus (also a triple-header) guards the gates of hell.

Personally, I was more into creating chaos here on Earth, where I torched the Turkish countryside with devastating wildfire (courtesy of my goat head). Until I was slain by the hero Bellerophon, that is, riding to the rescue on Pegasus. It was ugly: he drove a lead spear down my throat, and I choked on molten lead melted by my own fiery breath. My legend lives on, though: even today the word chimera means something grotesque, fantastic, or imaginary.

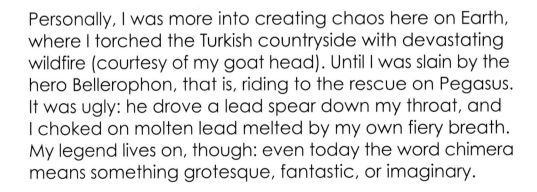

● The chimera is considered an omen of natural disasters, including volcanoes
● At Mount Chimera, in Turkey, gas seeps from rock and ignites flames
● In Greek mythology, the chimera is the sphinx's mother

Chimera

Hellhound
■ Four-Legged Beasts

✳ This spectral black dog features in tales from Great Britain
✳ Sometimes described as floating on a carpet of fog or mist
✳ Aka black shuck, barguest, moddey dhoo, gytrash, gurt dog

Bad dog? You bet! I'm a mangy black hound with a mean glint in my smoldering, saucer-sized red eyes. I'm a roamer, too—no spiked choke collar can restrain me, no fence can contain me. I've marked my territory over centuries of wandering—graveyards, crossroads, gallows hills, lonely country lanes. Look me in the eye and my gaze will burn right through you. My scent? It's sulfurous.

In 1577, in England, I appeared in a clap of thunder at the Church of Saint Mary in Bungay, Suffolk. I caused the choir inside to go way off key—right before the steeple buckled. Mayhem accomplished, I bounded on to Blythburgh Church, where the ruckus continued. I didn't just scratch the church doors, I scorched them. The sooty slash marks are there to this day.

● Early accounts of the hellhound date from the 1127 *Anglo-Saxon Chronicle*
● It appears in many stories, including *Hound of the Baskervilles* and *Jane Eyre*
● If spotted at the grave of a priest, it meant the priest had betrayed his vows

Hellhound

Pooka
■ Four-Legged Beasts

✳ A shape-shifting animal from Celtic mythology
✳ Often takes the form of a wild horse hung with chains
✳ Lures weary travelers for a romp they won't forget

Are you ready to risk your neck? Feel the breeze chill your marrow? Climb on for a breathtaking ride. Literally! What do you say? Will a ride on me be worth the rodeo?

In the days when traveling meant trudging along steep and rocky ways with a heavy pack, I haunted the night roads toward home, a sleek black steed with glowing amber eyes and the power of speech. A ride for the weary was enough to tempt tired travelers up on my back, but that's when the fun began. Off I went, leaping over gullies, galloping over stony ground, bucking in the moonlight. I had a long and flowing mane to grab onto, yet no one could control me. No one except the high king of Ireland Brian Boru, that is. He brought me right back down to earth with the aid of a bridle braided with hairs from my tail.

● Legend has it that if rain falls on a sunny day, the pooka will appear that night
● Different versions are found in Cornwall (pucca) and in Wales (pwca)
● The Cheval Mallet, a French cousin, throws its rider over cliffs

Pooka

Sphinx
■ Four-Legged Beasts

✸ A mythogical creature from ancient Egypt and Greece
✸ The Egyptian form has a lion's body and a man's head
✸ The Greek form has a lion's body, a woman's head, and wings

I recline calmly on my hind legs, my massive lion's paws outstretched. No need to growl or ambush when you've got a gaze as unnerving as mine. Unlike creatures who roar or rampage, I am never portrayed on the attack. Although in Greek myth I was famous for asking a riddle, the sound of my voice is a mystery.

In Egypt, I wear a *nemes* with a serpent symbol, the headdress of the pharaohs, and I guard the rulers' tombs and temples. In Greece, I was sentinel at the mountain pass to the city of Thebes. I played a pitiless game in which I ate those who could not answer this riddle: What has one voice, yet becomes four footed, then two footed, then three footed? Can you work it out? King Oedipus did, so I turned my revenge on myself, leaping from a rock to die.

● The Egyptian Great Sphinx of Giza dates from approximately 2500 BCE
● Sphinx probably comes from Greek *sphingein*, meaning "to bend or squeeze"
● The answer to the riddle is: man—as a baby, an adult, then old, with a cane

Sphinx

Unicorn
■ Four-Legged Beasts

* ✳ Opalescent horse-type creature with a single horn
* ✳ Some versions have a curly beard and a lion's tail
* ✳ Cousins include the Chinese ch'i lin and the Arab karkadann

Like the spiraling grooves in my horn, my tale has spun out over millennia. In 4 BCE, Ctesias, a Greek doctor, described a horsey creature from India with a horn that could be carved into magic goblets that were proof against any poison. Today, I'm considered pretty and pearlescent; back then, Ctesias described my head as dark red and my horn as black and white with a flame-red tip!

During the Middle Ages, I was hunted for my horn, as kings considered it to be a valuable rarity. Catching me is not easy—I am fleet and use my horn as a lance to fend off pursuing hounds. But I cannot resist a young maiden, especially one holding a mirror for me to gaze into. I'm too busy admiring myself to see the approaching hunters over my shoulder. Vanity is my downfall!

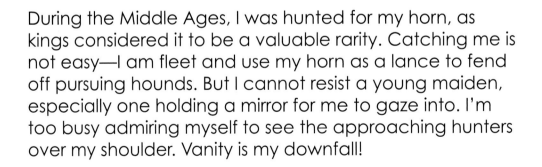

* ● In myth, forest animals relied on the unicorn to test streams for safety and purity
* ● 18th-century apothecaries supposedly kept unicorn horn among their medicines
* ● The UK coat of arms features a lion for England and a unicorn for Scotland

Unicorn

Cadejo
■ Four-Legged Beasts

❉ Ghostly, calf-sized dogs with origins in Central America
❉ They appear to travelers and can be black or white
❉ Evil ones drag chains; kind ones eat flowers on volcano slopes

Looking for company on a hazardous journey? I'm happy to oblige. Moving as nimbly as a deer in great bounding leaps, I'll scout for dangers that lie ahead. Let my glowing purple eyes light your way through the eerie night. The heat of my gaze is like smoldering lava; no surprise—I am a spirit child of Central American volcanoes and live inside their peaks. The country folk who inhabit the volcano slopes are my special care. I'll turn into a sudden wind to sweep a child safely away from a hidden crater.

Be warned, though—some of my pack have gone over to the dark side. They are easy to recognize: their hooved feet are shackled in molten chains, and they stink like a heap of garbage in the sun. When they die, they leave behind a stain that can never be cleaned.

● The name comes from Spanish *cadena* (chain) after the chains of evil cadejos
● In some tales, cadejos conduct people to the afterlife
● Turning away from an evil cadejo is said to drive a person insane

Cadejo

Nian
■ Four-Legged Beasts

✳ Monster associated with Chinese New Year celebrations
✳ Has an ox's body, a flat face, gaping mouth, and fangs
✳ Shies away from the color red and firecrackers

Hey! I demand respect! Where is the terror? The trepidation? Stop this New Year partying and go huddle in your huts everyone, or your children and grain fields are toast! I'm a monster, NOT an excuse for fun!

In ancient times, every new year, I crawled out of my undersea lair and raided a town. Villagers cowered in their huts or hid in the mountains. Any person still on the street or livestock left in the field went straight into my gaping gob. Then an old monk revealed that I feared the color red and the crackle of firecrackers. Villagers began setting off fireworks, dressing in red, and hanging red lanterns on their doors. These abominations became Chinese New Year traditions, and my yearly feasts turned to famines. Hmmm, life for a modern monster is stressful.

● The Chinese New Year marks the time in spring to start preparing to sow grain
● The large colorful puppets seen in Chinese New Year lion dances represent nian
● *Guo nian* means both "survive the nian" and "celebrate the new year"

Nian

Chapter 5
Spirits and Demons

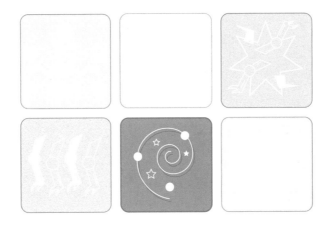

We're either decaying (Zombie), withered (Baba Yaga), ragged (Banshee), or rank (Windigo). Find yourself in our long-clawed clutches, and things won't go well for you. But Banshee will mourn your passing in song and Boggart will provide a few naughty noises at the funeral to cheer things up. We can deliver seasonal doom: wintry Windigo can freeze you in your tracks, or sunny siren Poludnica can fry you in the field. Your pick—we aim to make disaster a pleasure for our prey! If we like you, we can call on Fairy to grant you a wish—or maybe even lead you to a secret stash of fairy butter hidden in the woods.

Zombie

Baba Yaga

Banshee

Poludnica

Fairy

Goblin

Boggart

Windigo

Zombie
■ Spirits and Demons

✳ Walking dead body from Caribbean myth
✳ Zombies are ravenous for human flesh
✳ The word "zombie" may come from Bantu *nzúmbe* (ghost)

Undead? For sure. Zombie world is one go-go graveyard. I've got moldy, peeling skin, a shuffling, lumbering gait, and a mindless, wall-eyed stare. And, of course, the munchies for fresh human flesh snacks.

My African roots go deep. Nbzambi was a great West African spirit, the soul of the people. Enslaved Africans in the Caribbean endured a brutal life working on sugar plantations. They developed a religion of voodoo, merging African traditions with Christian beliefs. Dark sorcerers, *bocors*, could steal a person's soul, leaving just a human shell, or zombie. In Haiti, the religion became a form of resistance against the French slave masters. When freedom came, in 1791, the Haitians continued to fear zombies because the horror of enslavement was so hard to forget.

● *Bocors* created zombies using a magic potion said to contain puffer fish poison
● Prehistoric cultures may have used gravestones to keep the dead in their graves
● An undead being in Tibet is known as a *ro-lang*—"the corpse who stands up"

Zombie

Baba Yaga
■ Spirits and Demons

✳ A witchlike character from Eastern European folklore
✳ *Baba* means "old woman"; *yaga* may mean "shudder"
✳ Flies through the sky in a mortar, using a pestle to steer

Call me witchy, I won't mind in the least! It's a hoot to be an old hag. For one thing, I'm free to look any old witch-way I like—and I do: scrawny knock-knees? Check. A nose so long it scrapes the ceiling when I lie down? Check. (Is there a wart on it? You bet!) Iron teeth? Check. Do they need whitening? Nah, I just hone the rust off with a nice sharp human bone shard from the spikes on my garden fence.

And my hag's hut? It's got all the latest crone-cottage updates! Raised safely off the forest floor on chicken legs, it auto-rotates so the spy-cam windows can zoom in on little lost children wandering around the forest floor. Parked in my yard, my mortar with three-speed auto-pestle gears is a sweet ride through the sky on a stormy night.

● It is said that Baba Yaga can remove her hands to send them on errands
● In stories, she sets tasks for children and eats the ones who fail to fulfill them
● In one popular tale, Vasilisa, a maiden who completes the tasks, is set free

Baba Yaga

Banshee
■ Spirits and Demons

※ In Irish folklore, a female spirit whose cry signals a family death
※ Thought to be the spirit of a deceased ancestor
※ The name means "woman of the fairy mound"

We are divas of death. We sing you to eternal sleep, but our songs are laments, not lullabies. In Irish, we are the *bean-sidhe*, female death messengers draped in ragged shrouds. Eyes red with weeping, we tear out our hair and send our shrieks and wails out on the wind. Irish families know that our songs are a portent that the death of a family member is nigh. We foretell death but do not cause it.

In medieval times, we crouched in shallow streams, wailing as we washed the bloody armor of a knight doomed to die in battle. At the cottages of peasants or castles of the great, we sent our cries down the chimney or through a chink in the window of the bedchamber of the doomed one. Barley cakes were said to have appeased us but not for long. Like a cold draft, we always found our way in.

- Families of pure Irish blood had their own personal banshee
- Laments were said to whisper the name of the person whose death was due
- A comb found on the ground might belong to a banshee; it's bad luck to touch it

Banshee

Poludnica

■ Spirits and Demons

※ A harvesttime spirit from Slavic folklore
※ Appears to farmhands during the heat of the day
※ Name comes from Polish *poludnie* (noon or midday)

Feeling the midday heat? Let me take you out of the hot sun and into the cool, dim shade. Just one warning, I'm talking about a shady rest that lasts forever.

Watch for me when the heat rises in the fields, kicking up dust in a swirly cyclone. I'll appear as it whirls, no mirage, just a pretty lady in a long white dress, my wheat-colored hair ruffled by the breeze. I'll have a riddle for you. Answer correctly and you'll come to no harm. Stumped? See that sickle I'm carrying? I will strike you down. Or perhaps I will make you see a watery pool in the distance—a welcome release from the searing heat. Go ahead, crawl toward it. But watch out! Instead of a lifesaving, cool drink all you'll find is a heat mirage. That midday sun must be feeling really suffocating by now . . .

● This myth was used as a threat to stop children playing in valuable grain fields
● Some victims went mad, an allusion to mental confusion caused by heatstroke
● Czech composer Antonin Dvorak wrote a symphony based on the legend

Poludnica

Fairy
■ Spirits and Demons

✳ Mythical being from the folklore of many European cultures
✳ First described as having an "astral" body, like a cloud
✳ Aka the gentry, fair folk, good neighbors, and *sidhe* (hill folk)

In olden times, humans searching for "the gentry" would listen for strange music on the wind or watch for fairy lights at twilight. They left us milk poured into the crevices of stones. Those with second sight could see us playing under sacred trees—hazel, blackthorn, or elder. We might disappear in an instant, our bodies as airy as clouds.

So, humans, why do you now pave our age-old grassy tracks with sticky tar? We like to dance there! Why do you bulldoze the earthen barrows that protect our hill homes? Don't you know we'll take revenge? We can lead travelers astray by making landmarks disappear. Or perhaps we'll steal a human baby, leaving a fairy baby in its place. Remember: we share the land with you. Treat it gently and you will be safe from our anger.

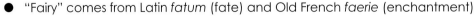

● "Fairy" comes from Latin *fatum* (fate) and Old French *faerie* (enchantment)
● The Victorians popularized the image of fairies as tiny winged sprites
● Red thread tied around the wrist or neck is a protection against fairy magic

Fairy

Goblin
■ Spirits and Demons

✳ Mean and mischievous creature from European folklore
✳ A scavenger that lives in a lair inside a mountain
✳ Travels in hordes, raiding peaceful towns

Light, air, sunshine—pfaugh! We goblins find all that freshness just too foul! We'd rather be in a stuffy tunnel bored deep into the mountains. We have sickly greenish skin and long, scrawny fingers good for gripping the necks of our victims or grasping any riches that come our way. Our only weakness is our feet. They're tender due to constant exposure to dampness and slime, so we wear iron or stone boots to protect them.

We make battle gear—helmets, pikes, clubs—from iron ore, silver, or any material that can be mined. We don't grow our food, we snatch it, grabbing bugs from tunnel walls, rats from the rubbish heaps, and eyeless fish from the stagnant pools in our caverns. We like to make war on humans—what better chance to test our weapons?

● Mountain lairs are littered with bones and the carcasses of small animals
● In Harry Potter, goblins are talented bankers, capable of wandless magic
● J. R. R. Tolkien's goblins are the great enemies of wizards

Goblin

Boggart
■ Spirits and Demons

✳ Household troublemaker from England
✳ Treated respectfully, a boggart will sometimes do chores
✳ Aka nippen, nick, boggle, lubber-fiend, bwgan (Wales)

Rude and cheeky, I'm a naughty word come to life, complete with embarrassing noises. Pppppttttttffffk! You're wondering who did that? Well, I did, but I'm just a puff of breeze stirring the curtains, so don't go pointing a finger! In your house, I inhabit all the little notches and niches that you don't notice, like that snug little pipe bend under the bathroom sink (I've got a cozy nest in the mold there) or that downy-soft dust bunny under your bed.

When I venture outdoors, I loiter in sharp turns in the road to make you tumble from your bike or in driveway mud puddles where your homework decides to drop. And if your pony kicks up its heels, spilling you in the dirt, it might have something to do with the burr I sneaked under its saddle. That's pure Boggart possession!

● Old English manor houses often have their own resident boggart
● Boggarts enjoy pulling blankets off sleeping people and souring milk
● In Harry Potter, boggarts take the shape of their victims' worst fears

Boggart

Windigo
■ Spirits and Demons

✳ Evil spirit of the native Algonquian peoples of North America
✳ Created by being bitten by a windigo, or by a shaman's spell
✳ Aka witigo, atuush (East Cree tribe), chenoo (Mi'kmaq tribe)

A human driven wild by famine, I am an ashen-faced, purple-lipped creature that hunts under the moon of late winter. I'm thirsty for the warm bloody juice of what was once my own kind, before my human feelings were bitten by frost and my heart turned to ice. No longer civilized, without care for tribe or family, I've tossed the taboo against cannibalism to the winter wind. I have the primitive strength of a ravenous predator and will do whatever it takes to beat starvation.

No longer able to speak in words, my voice now sounds like the crack of a dead tree branch in the frigid air or the gutteral bark of a fox. I've grown a great rack of horns, and I have feet of fire. My flesh is festering and fetid, and I give off the rank stink of someone rotten to the core.

● The windigo is symbolic of winter, hunger, and selfishness
● In some tales, cooking kettles are used to trick or lure windigos and kill them
● A silver bullet will kill a windigo, but its icy heart must be removed and melted

Windigo

Chapter 6
Almost Human

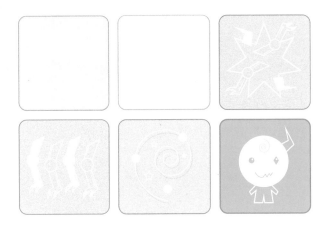

Almost human, huh? Don't insult us! Sure, we might have a few somewhat human features—Centaur and Minotaur have muscular arms good for grappling with enemies, and Troll has a substantial-sized snoot perfect for sniffing out his next victim. But any similarities have to stop there. Our homes, for example, are not fit for human habitation! Would you like to live like Minotaur, in a labyrinth littered with dead bodies and with no exit? Or Troll, he lives under a leaky bridge—nothing fancy about that! Vampire tries to keep up appearances with his cloaks and his castles, but come on, the guy makes his bed in a coffin!

Centaur

Minotaur

Brownie

Troll

Gnome

Vampire

Werewolf

Centaur
■ Almost Human

* Half man, half horse creature from Greek mythology
* Some centaur tribes were calmer and wiser than others
* Centaur means "bull killer"; Greeks hunted bulls on horseback

Think twice before you invite me to any weddings! I have a reputation for kicking up my heels at parties. My dad Centaurus mated with Magnesian mares, and so a whole herd of us was born, and we've been running wild in the mountainous forests of Thessaly, in Greece, ever since! Our mixed parentage is reflected in our appearance—human to the waist with horse hindquarters.

To our shame, we can't hold our wine. At the wedding of our half-brother, Pirithous, we got drunk and tried to abduct the bride and the bridesmaids, too! Pirithous's best bud, the hero Theseus, was not amused. The rip-roaring battle that ensued is known as the Centauromachy, and despite our best efforts (we uprooted oak trees to use as weapons), many of us were slain.

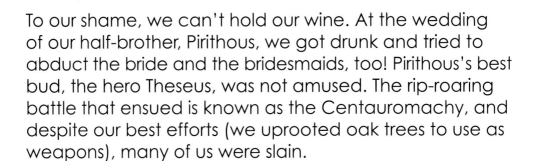

● Civilized centaurs had human forelegs and a horse rear joined at the waist
● A wise centaur, Chiron, taught the Greek heroes Achilles and Hercules
● Female centaurs were called centaurides and had coats like chestnut mares

Centaur

Minotaur
■ Almost Human

✳ Hybrid creature from ancient Greek mythology
✳ A bull's head, horns, and tail with a human body and limbs
✳ Minotaur means "bull of Minos"

Sometimes families don't get along, but mine . . . whew! My tale is as twisted as the labyrinth that became my prison. My mother, Queen Pasiphae of Crete, nursed me, but as I grew, I became ferocious. That was my bull nature—my father was a pure white bull sent by the god Poseidon as a sign of favor to my stepfather, King Minos. When Minos didn't sacrifice the bull to Poseidon as he had promised, Poseidon made my mom fall in love with it.

Embarrassed by my birth, King Minos imprisoned me in a labyrinth designed by the architect Daedalus. My family's idea of a homey meal was to feed me Athenian youths— they just tossed them down the maze hatch. When the hero Theseus killed me with his club, some say I barely fought back. I mean, who were the monsters here?

● Queen Pasiphae named the minotaur Asterion (Starry One)
● Theseus used a magic thread to help trace his way through the labyrinth
● The famous artist Pablo Picasso created many works based on the legend

Minotaur

Brownie
■ Almost Human

☀ Small human-type creature (usually male) of Scottish origin
☀ Has wrinkled skin, curly hair, and is dressed in brown rags
☀ The guardian of a particular homestead, family, or lineage

Brownie Inc. here, the firm to call for household help. But before we start work, let's discuss the terms of our employment. No griping about our fashion choices! Our tattered togs are sooty and smudged. We sweep your hearths and empty your dustbins—a little dirt is part of the deal! Try to tart us up and we'll take offense and quit the premises. We don't do servant livery! Are we agreed?

Now let's talk about meal plans. Farm to table works for us! We like a bowl of the sweetest brose (that's porridge to you), left to warm on the hearth, please! So what's in it for you? Well, we'll mow your fields, clean your barns, wash your pans, and churn your butter. If you fuss about the quality of our work, though, here's mud in your eye: we're known for throwing clods of dirt.

● Gruagach were brownies who lived in the Hebrides and watched flocks
● In Cornwall, brownies were said to make swarming bees settle quickly
● The hook used to hang pots over open hearths was known as a brownie's seat

Brownie

Troll
■ Almost Human

☀ Nocturnal humanoid from Scandinavian tradition
☀ Has a humpback, long ears and nose, and stumpy legs
☀ In Norse tradition, the word *trolleri* refers to "menacing magic"

Like a massive boulder come to lumpy life, I blend easily into the sunless underground lairs where I prefer to lurk. Caves, under bridges, mountain caverns, mineshafts— these dank digs are home to me, because when I am exposed to sunlight, I turn to stone. In war, I have the brute strength of a battering ram and can pluck trees from the earth to hurl as missiles.

I love to eat. At gatherings, we trolls argue endlessly about the best way to cook our victims (human, hobbit, dwarf, or goblin): should we boil them, roast them, or bake them in a pie? Our meals are always washed down by plenty of strong mead, which we store in stone crocks. The washing up? Not our strong point. We just smash the crockery after a meal—that is, if we bother to use it at all.

● Trolls are always pagan; ringing churchbells will drive a troll away
● J. R. R. Tolkien's *The Lord of the Rings* features cave, hill, and mountain trolls
● Internet "trolls" purposely post content to create conflict and division

Troll

Gnome
■ Almost Human

☀ Short, bearded, humanoid creature of European origin
☀ Wears a leather tool belt, a colorful tunic, and a stocking cap
☀ Name probably derives from Greek *genomos* (earth dweller)

We read the writing on the garden wall: specialize! In the competitive world of mischievous household spirits, we decided to make a name for ourselves as groundskeeping experts. It has worked for us: estimates put the world gnome population at 25 million.

Long ago we were associated with mines, but we opted to surrender that territory to dwarves and goblins, though we do dabble in precious gem cutting. With all the healthful exercise that we get planting, weeding, and pruning, no surprise that we are long-lived: Lampy, our beloved elder gnome, is over 150 years old and even survived a pitiless gnome purge carried out by the heirs of England's Lamport Hall. They considered garden gnomes in poor taste! Stay strong, Lampy: gnome power!

● Gnomes eat herbs, mushrooms, garden vegetables, berries, and nuts
● The Gnome Reserve In Devon, England, is tended by more than 2,000 gnomes
● In Harry Potter, gnomes are garden pests who bite and look a bit like potatoes

Gnome

Vampire
■ Almost Human

☀ Reanimated corpse of European tradition
☀ Rises from the grave at night to drink the blood of the living
☀ A stake driven through the heart is said to kill a vampire

Blood is my beverage of choice, of course, but—family secret—some of my relatives chew shrouds, the cloths that wrap corpses! In fiction, I'm a debonair demon with cape, cravat, and greased-back hair, a Eurotrash title (Count), and a Carpathian castle. Its stone ramparts are perfect for my night crawls in search of a snack.

I suffer from arithmomania. Toss a handful of mustard seeds in my path and I'll stop to count them while you make your escape. Other things that repel me? Hawthorn and rowan branches, garlic, peppermint, and running water. My association with Eastern European nobility dates to my ancestor, Vlad the Impaler, a 15th-century Wallachian prince who dipped his bread in the blood of his torture victims. Bon appetit, dear cousin Vlad!

● Unburied bodies jumped over by cats are said to turn into vampires
● In medieval times, vampires were blamed for spreading deadly diseases
● Bela Lugosi, who once portrayed Count Dracula, was buried in full costume

Vampire

Werewolf
■ Almost Human

* A shape-shifting wolf man from European lore
* Undergoes transformation by the light of a full moon
* The name comes from Old English *wer* (man) plus wolf

Do I look a bit hangdog to you? A little gnarly or snarly? Not to whine, but compared to other shape-shifters, I go through some brutal transitions. Popping out in paws, claws, facial fur, and fangs—then back again—is a drag, I can tell you. Darn that full moon!

You see, I'm not in control of my changing, it just happens when the moon is full. I may be tricked into wolf form by trying out a magic ointment or an enchanted wolf pelt found in the woods. Once snagged, I'm doomed to an endless push and pull between my wolf and human shapes and natures. Sometimes I maul people I love, and when the moon changes, I slink away in shame. Back in human form, I feel guilty about my deeds! But on the night of the next full moon—aroooohhh! . . . I move in for the kill again!

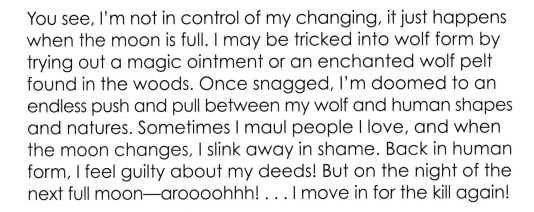

● In medieval times, werewolves were wolves with a rational human nature
● In modern lore, they look part human (two legs) but have a wolfish nature
● In Norse sagas, wearing a magic wolf pelt turned a man into a wolf for 10 days

Werewolf

Index

Glossary

Alchemist A person who practices a medieval version of chemistry that studied how to turn ordinary matter into precious substances.

Amphibious Able to live both on land and in water.

Antidote A remedy that reverses or lessens the effects of poison.

Apothecary A store or collection of remedies.

Arithmomania An abnormal compulsion to count things or make mathematical calculations.

Astral Of, or related to, the stars or heavens. The term can be used to describe a nonphysical, spiritual being.

Bestiary A collection of descriptions or illustrations of real or imaginary animals.

Carnivore An animal that feeds mostly on the flesh of other animals.

Cryptozoology The search for, and study of, animals whose existence has not been proven by science.

Demigod A minor divine being, such as the child of a god and a human being.

Dissonant A sound combination that clashes and lacks harmony.

Echolocation The process by which certain animals, such as bats and dolphins, use sound waves reflected back from objects in space to help them navigate their way around.

Elusive Difficult to find, catch, hold, or understand.

Fetid A penetrating, foul smell, especially from something rotten.

Hominid A member of a primate group that includes humans, gorillas, and chimps.

Humanoid A nonhuman creature with characteristics resembling those of a human being (such as the ability to walk upright).

Hybrid A creature whose body is made up of several parts from different animals.

Immortal A being that lives forever, that does not die. The term is often used when talking about gods and goddesses.

Luminous Emitting or reflecting a steady, usually glowing or softly bright, light.

Maritime Connected to the sea. The term is especially used in relation to seafaring and sailors.

Omen An event or creature that is a forewarning, sign, or signal of something to come in the future.

Omnivore An animal that feeds on both plants and the flesh of other animals.

Opalescent/Pearlescent
When the surface of an object or substance shimmers with colors—like an opal or pearl.

Predator An animal that hunts down other creatures.

Primate A member of the most developed group of mammals, including humans and apes.

Regenerate To reform, regrow, or replace lost or injured tissue, limb, organ, etc.

Rheumy Watery, blurry, cloudy, discharging fluid or mucus, usually referring to the eyes.

Saga A long, involved, or complicated story. The term is especially associated with the Norse myths.

Shaman A priest or priestess who uses magic to contact and/or influence the spirit world.

Shape-shifter A mythical or folkloric creature with the ability to transform or shift from one physical form to another.

Spectral Ghostly, like a spirit or phantom.

Stagnant Stale, sluggish, often smelly, without movement or flow. The term usually refers to water.